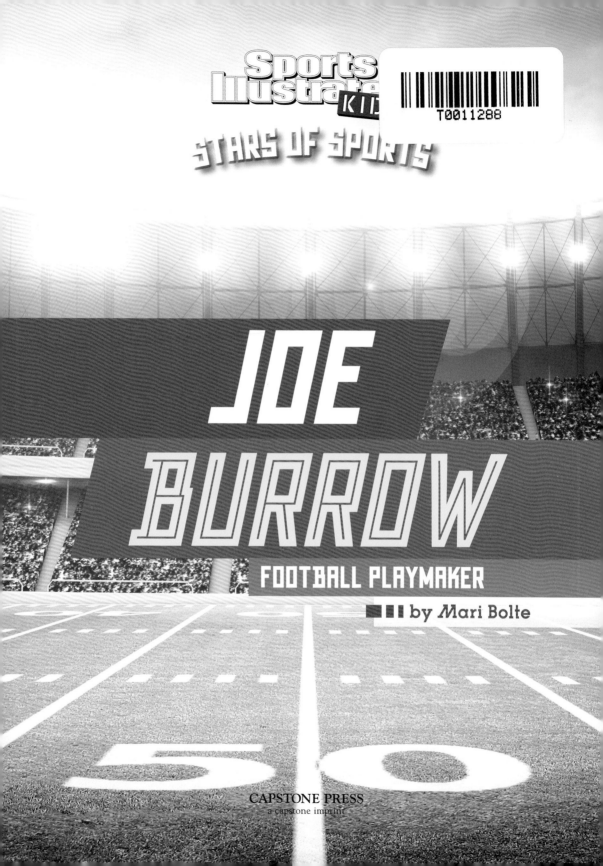

Sports Illustrated KIDS

STARS OF SPORTS

JOE BURROW

FOOTBALL PLAYMAKER

by Mari Bolte

CAPSTONE PRESS
a capstone imprint

Published by Capstone Press, an imprint of Capstone
1710 Roe Crest Drive, North Mankato, Minnesota 56003
capstonepub.com

Library of Congress Cataloging-in-Publication Data
Names: Bolte, Mari, author.
Title: Joe Burrow : football playmaker / by Mari Bolte.
Description: North Mankato, Minnesota : Capstone Press, an imprint of Capstone, [2024] | Series: Sports illustrated kids stars of sports | Includes bibliographical references and index. | Audience: Ages 8 to 11 | Audience: Grades 4-6 | Summary: "Young star quarterback Joe Burrow is a born football playmaker. He fought back from a serious injury his rookie season to take his team to he Super Bowl the next year. Burrow has impressed teammates, coaches, and fans with his determination and strong work ethic. Get more details about his journey to NFL stardom"— Provided by publisher.
Identifiers: LCCN 2022053017 (print) | LCCN 2022053018 (ebook) | ISBN 9781669018339 (hardcover) | ISBN 9781669018285 (paperback) | ISBN 9781669018292 (pdf) | ISBN 9781669018315 (kindle edition) | ISBN 9781669018322 (epub)
Subjects: LCSH: Burrow, Joe, 1996- —Juvenile literature. | Quarterbacks (Football)—United States—Biography—Juvenile literature.
Classification: LCC GV939.B873 B65 2024 (print) | LCC GV939.B873 (ebook) | DDC 796.332092 [B]—dc23/eng/20221102
LC record available at https://lccn.loc.gov/2022053017
LC ebook record available at https://lccn.loc.gov/2022053018

Editorial Credits
Editor: Mandy Robbins; Designer: Hilary Wacholz; Media Researcher: Jo Miller; Production Specialist: Tori Abraham

Image Credits
Associated Press: Aaron M. Sprecher via AP, 14, AP Photo/Aaron Doster, 20, AP Photo/Athens Messenger, Louise Fish, 9, AP Photo/Emilee Chinn, 7, AP Photo/Jason Szenes, 13, Cal Sport Media via AP Images, 10, 12, 15, Icon Sportswire via AP Images, 11, 17, 21, 23, 25, Keith Birmingham/The Orange County Register via AP, 26, Logan Bowles via AP, 16, Michael Owens via AP, 28, NFL via AP, 18, Ryan Kang via AP, 27; Shutterstock: EFKS, 1; Sports Illustrated: Erick W. Rasco, cover, 5

Source Notes
Pg. 8: "I knew [he was special]. . ." Joe Grobeck, "Joe Burrow's High School Coach Shares the Greatness He Saw in Him at 15," FanBuzz, February 4, 2022, https://fanbuzz.com/nfl/joe-burrow-high-school-coach/, accessed May 30, 2022.
Pg. 11: ". . . it was kind of a culture shock . . ." Bill Bender, "Why Didn't Joe Burrow Start at Ohio State? Revisiting His Transfer to LSU," The Sporting News, February 13, 2022, https://www.sportingnews.com/us/ncaa-football/news/joe-burrow-ohio-state-transfer-lsu/wxyjktgmysiuf0mdbxrhqfnj, accessed May 30, 2022.
Pg. 19: "I've won everywhere . . ." Jordan Dajani, "Five NFL Teams that Could Be Better Than You Expect in 2022: Dolphins and Saints Poised to Make Some Noise," CBSSports.com, May 27, 2022, https://www.cbssports.com/nfl/news/five-nfl-teams-that-could-be-better-than-you-expect-in-2022-dolphins-and-saints-poised-to-make-some-noise/, accessed May 30, 2022.
Pg. 19: "Enough talk. Time to get to work." Joe Burrow, Twitter, https://twitter.com/joeyb/status/1253482947358920704, Accessed May 30, 2022.
Pg. 21: "Thanks for all the love . . ." NFL Game Highlights, "'The Season': The 2021 Bengals' Remarkable Run to Super Bowl LVI," NFL, https://www.nfl.com/videos/the-season-the-21-bengals-remarkable-run-to-super-bowl-lvi, accessed May 30, 2022.
Pg. 22: "He'll be ready . . ." Jason Marcum, "Update on Joe Burrow's Recovery Timeline," SB Nation: Cincy Jungle, November 23, 2020, https://www.cincyjungle.com/2020/11/23/21611434/joe-burrow-recovery-timeline-acl-mcl-tear-injury-bengals-news, accessed May 30, 2022.
Pg. 24: "You guys asked me early . . ." Charlie Goldsmith, "Cincinnati Bengals beat Minnesota Vikings in NFL Week 1 after OT drama," Cincinnati Enquirer, September 12, 2021, https://www.cincinnati.com/story/sports/nfl/bengals/2021/09/12/cincinnati-bengals-vs-minnesota-vikings-nfl-week-1-score-updates/8303480002/, accessed May 30, 2022.
Pg. 28: "His standard is greatness . . ." Charlie Goldsmith, "Joe Burrow, Patrick Mahomes and the Future of the Quarterback Position in the NFL," Cincinnati Enquirer, January 26, 2022, https://www.cincinnati.com/story/sports/nfl/bengals/2022/01/26/joe-burrow-and-patrick-mahomes-represent-nfl-quarterbacks-future/9211079002/, accessed May 30, 2022.

TABLE OF CONTENTS

Words in **BOLD** are in the glossary.

THE ROAD TO THE SUPER BOWL

On January 15, 2022, quarterback Joe Burrow had something to prove. He and his team, the Cincinnati Bengals, were in the **wild card** game of the National Football League (NFL) **playoffs**. It was his first postseason start. It was just his second year in the NFL. A win would put the team on the path to the Super Bowl.

The Las Vegas Raiders scored three points early in the game. But Burrow answered. The Bengals' first turn with the ball was a 10-play, 75-yard drive. It led to a touchdown. The next four possessions were point-earners too. Burrow passed for 244 yards. He threw two touchdowns. The Bengals won the game with a final score of 26–19.

It was the first time the Bengals had won a playoff game since 1991. That was the longest time without a playoff win in the NFL. With Burrow as their quarterback, the Bengals would go on to become the American Football Conference (AFC) Champions. They would play in Super Bowl LVI.

〉〉〉 Burrow prepares to throw the ball in the 2022 wild card game.

CHAPTER ONE

BORN TO PLAY

Joseph Lee Burrow was born in Ames, Iowa, on December 10, 1996. His father, Jimmy, had been a professional football player. He was also a college football coach. Joe's mother, Robin, was a school principal. The Burrow family moved a lot. Jimmy's coaching job sent them to Nebraska, then to North Dakota. Finally, they landed in Ohio in 2005.

Joe's older brothers, Jamie and Dan, played football too. They played in college for Nebraska. Their uncle John had played for Ole Miss. Sports were in the Burrow blood. Joe would have that same talent.

>>> Burrow's parents cheer for him and the Bengals during a 2020 game against the Cleveland Browns.

FACT

On October 23, 2022, Burrow became the first NFL quarterback to have more than one game with 500 yards and four touchdowns.

When Burrow was in third grade, he started playing youth football. His coach knew the Burrow family history. He made Burrow the quarterback.

Burrow could come up with plays on his own. If there was no one open, he would run the ball in himself. When he was in 10th grade, he earned the starting quarterback spot. "I knew [he was special] after the first game," his high school coach said later. "Joe was a 15-year-old sophomore . . . in his first game he made it look like he had been doing it for years."

Burrow led his high school to the playoffs three times in a row. Joe started his senior year as the seventh-best quarterback in Ohio's history. He threw for more than 11,000 passing yards. He threw 63 touchdowns and only two **interceptions** during his senior year.

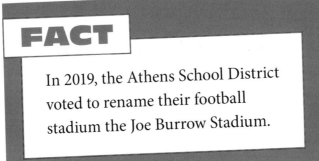

FACT

In 2019, the Athens School District voted to rename their football stadium the Joe Burrow Stadium.

>>> Burrow throws a pass for his high school team in a 2014 game.

CHAPTER TWO

PLAYING COLLEGE BALL

By 2014, Burrow knew he wanted to play college football. He was a senior. He was ready to reach the next level. But not many players in his area were playing for top colleges. **Recruiters** didn't want to take the time to travel to a small town in Ohio. Ohio University, where Jimmy coached, sent him an offer. But Burrow didn't take it seriously. He felt like the offer was related to his dad, not his skill. He kept waiting for another offer to come along.

〉〉〉 Burrow warming up before a 2017 Buckeyes game

Finally, the Ohio State Buckeyes took an interest in Joe. Then other schools noticed. More offers came in. But they didn't matter to Burrow. He was set on being a Buckeye.

Going from a small town to a huge college was something Burrow didn't expect. ". . . it was kind of a culture shock when I got to Ohio State and realized how good everybody was," he said. He worked hard but was never given a starting position. Then in 2017, he broke his hand in practice. There were two other good quarterbacks on the team. Burrow's time at Ohio State was over.

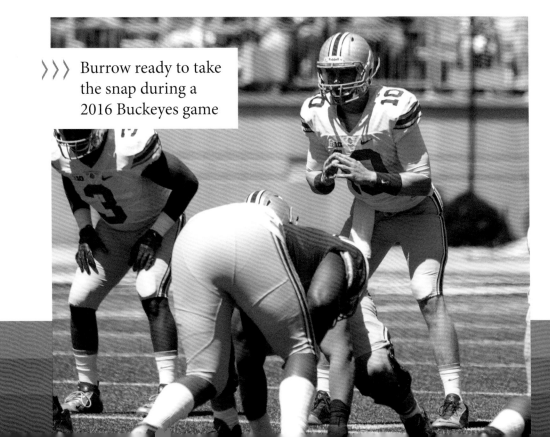

〉〉〉 Burrow ready to take the snap during a 2016 Buckeyes game

In May 2018, Burrow transferred to Louisiana State University (LSU). Finally, he got to be a starter. He ended the season with 2,894 passing yards and 16 touchdowns. It looked like the LSU Tigers had a new quarterback.

In 2019, LSU made it to the Southeastern Conference's (SEC) championship game. It was the first time they had gotten that far since 2011. They hadn't won since 2007. In 2018, LSU's offense was rated 38th. With Burrow as quarterback, they were ranked number one. That was enough to earn Burrow the 2019 Heisman Trophy.

》》》 Burrow in action during a 2017 LSU game

The Heisman Trophy

Every year, the Heisman Memorial Trophy is awarded to the best college football player in the country. It gets its name from John W. Heisman. Heisman was a college football coach in the 1890s. He helped the game gain popularity around the country. The first Heisman Trophy was given in 1935.

A winner is chosen by voting. Ballots go out to members of the media in late November. Former winners get a vote too. They choose their favorite players. The top three to six are announced on December 3. The winner is announced days later. Burrow earned 90.7 percent of the vote—a Heisman record. He was only the second LSU player ever to win.

In the playoff semifinals on December 28, 2019, LSU played the University of Oklahoma. It was Burrow's first game after winning the Heisman. He would be facing the Heisman runner-up, Oklahoma's quarterback Jalen Hurts. The Tigers had not lost once. LSU fans had high hopes. Burrow met them all.

FACT

Burrow dedicated his Heisman acceptance speech to kids in his home county of Athens who struggled with hunger and **poverty**. Donations and fundraisers poured into the state.

〉〉〉 Jalen Hurts in action against LSU in 2019

During the game's first half, Burrow threw seven touchdowns. In total, he threw for 493 yards. He ran in another touchdown during the third quarter. The Tigers scored more points than any team in a playoff game. The final score was 63–28. LSU was on their way to the championships.

〉〉〉 Burrow throws a pass in the December 28, 2019 game against Oklahoma.

The college football championship was played on January 13, 2020. LSU played Clemson. Clemson's quarterback, future NFL star Trevor Lawrence, hadn't lost a game since he had played in high school. Clemson's team hadn't lost since the 2017–18 season.

None of that mattered to Burrow, though. He threw for 463 yards and six touchdowns. LSU scored a 42–25 win. They were the national college champions!

〉〉〉 Burrow runs for a touchdown against Clemson.

〉〉〉 Burrow celebrates with the championship trophy after defeating Clemson.

During the 2019–20 season, Burrow was named the **offensive** Most Valuable Player (MVP) for the national championship game. He also threw for his 60th career touchdown. With the national championship and the Heisman, Burrow was only the 16th player to win both in the same year.

CHAPTER THREE

GOING PRO

The NFL **Draft** was coming up. Usually, it is a huge event. Hundreds of thousands of fans go there. Because of the **COVID-19 pandemic**, the 2020 Draft was virtual. There would be no party. There would be no crowds. Instead, Burrow moved back to his parents' home in Athens to wait for the big day.

〉〉〉 Burrow attended the 2020 draft virtually.

Everyone knew Burrow would be a top pick. "I've won everywhere that I've been," he said. "I've never had a losing season in sports . . . I just wanna go somewhere where I can win."

He would have played anywhere. But he also felt he had something to prove. The Ohio State Buckeyes hadn't given him his shot. Playing for the Cincinnati Bengals would be a second chance to represent Ohio.

Burrow got that chance. He was drafted by the Bengals. And he was the number-one draft pick. "Enough talk," he tweeted afterward. "Time to get to work."

The NFL Draft

The NFL Draft is a three-day event held each spring. There are seven rounds. Each of the 32 NFL football teams gets one pick per round. The pick order is determined by that team's finish in the previous season. The team with the worst record picks first. Teams can also trade players and draft pick slots.

To be eligible for the draft, players must be at least three years out of high school. They also cannot play in college. Around 3,000 college players are considered every year. About 400 of them are picked. Those 400 must choose between staying in college and joining the NFL.

The Cincinnati Bengals didn't waste any of Burrow's time. His first game was opening week against the Los Angeles Chargers. He was the only **rookie** quarterback from his draft year to play. It was a season of ups and downs, but Burrow kept improving.

Then, on November 22, 2020, the Bengals played the Washington Football Team. Burrow dropped back for a pass. Two Washington linemen ran in to tackle him.

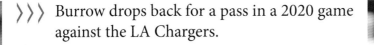

Burrow drops back for a pass in a 2020 game against the LA Chargers.

 Burrow gets help off the field after being injured.

There were no crowds in the stand because of the COVID-19 pandemic. Burrow's cry of pain as he was hit was the only sound. A cart came onto the field. Burrow was taken to the locker room. He had torn the ACL and MCL **ligaments** in his left leg. Burrow's rookie season was over.

"Thanks for all the love. Can't get rid of me that easy. See ya next year," Burrow tweeted.

FACT

The ACL and MCL are ligaments in the knee. They connect the thigh bone to the shin bone and also protect the knee joints.

No one knew when Burrow would be back to play. His injury had been serious. Similar accidents have sidelined players for as long as two years. Burrow had less than nine months to get better before the next season.

The fans were concerned. Reporters hounded Bengals head coach, Zac Taylor, for his opinion. But Taylor wasn't worried. He said, "He'll be ready for the 2021 season." When questioned, he said, "I've said what I said."

No one wanted to be back on the field more than Burrow. He worked hard at **rehab**. By December, he didn't need a cast or brace. In May, his doctor told reporters that Burrow would be on the field for the first snap of 2021.

>>> Burrow practicing in August 2021, wearing a knee brace

CHAPTER FOUR
BACK IN THE GAME

The Bengals started their 2021 season with Burrow in as quarterback. Even better, during the 2021 Draft, the Bengals had taken Burrow's former teammate, Ja'marr Chase. Chase and Burrow had been a winning combination at LSU. Fans were back in the stands to see the pair reunited.

During the first game, Burrow threw a 50-yard touchdown pass to Chase. He threw another for 32 yards to C.J. Uzomah in overtime. The team won their first game of the season against the Minnesota Vikings.

"You guys asked me early in the week how important the first game was and I kind of shrugged it off," Burrow admitted after the game. "But the first game is really important."

>>> Burrow steps back for a pass against the Minnesota Vikings in their 2021 game.

The Bengals made it to the 2021 NFL Playoffs with a 10–7 record. In the playoffs, they defeated the Las Vegas Raiders, the Tennessee Titans, and the Kansas City Chiefs. For the first time since 1988, the Bengals were headed to the Super Bowl.

More than 70,000 people came to watch Super Bowl LVI. Burrow would be head-to-head with the Los Angeles Rams' veteran quarterback, Matthew Stafford. It was an unexpected matchup. The Rams were playing on their home field. Football fans were excited to see new teams face off.

〉〉〉 Burrow gets sacked against the LA Rams.

The Bengals led most of the first half. As the second half began, Burrow threw for 75 yards to give the team a 17–13 lead. The Rams pressured Burrow. He was **sacked** five times in the third quarter alone. Burrow sprained his MCL but stayed in the game. With less than two minutes left, the Rams scored the winning touchdown. The game ended, 23-20.

〉〉〉 Outside linebacker Von Miller sacks Burrow.

CHAPTER FIVE

LOOKING TO THE FUTURE

Although the Bengals did not win the Super Bowl, they did better than anyone expected. During the 2020 season, the team had only four wins. No one knew if or when Burrow would return from his injury. And yet, just a year later, he led the team to a near win in the world's biggest football game. Burrow was named the 2021 Associated Press NFL Comeback Player of the Year.

Burrow has done exactly what the Bengals needed him to do. He was the fastest number-one-draft-pick quarterback to lead a team to a Super Bowl. "His standard is greatness," head coach Zac Taylor said. He and other young quarterbacks are the future of the NFL.

〉〉〉 Burrow accepting his award in 2021

TIMELINE

1996 Joseph Lee Burrow is born on December 10, in Ames, Iowa.

2005 The Burrow family moves to Athens, Ohio.

2012 Burrow earns the starting quarterback position on his high school team.

2015 Burrow enrolls at Ohio State University.

2018 Burrow transfers to Louisiana State University.

2019 LSU makes it to the college football playoffs.

2019 Burrow is awarded the Heisman Trophy.

2020 LSU plays Clemson in the college football championships on January 13.

2020 Burrow is chosen by the Cincinnati Bengals as the number-one pick during the NFL Draft.

2020 Burrow plays his first NFL game on September 13.

2020 Burrow takes a hit during the game against the Washington Football Team on November 22. He tears his ACL and MCL.

2021 Burrow gets a win during his first game back after his injury against the Minnesota Vikings on September 12.

2022 The Bengals beat the Las Vegas Raiders in the NFL wild card game on January 15.

2022 The Bengals play in Super Bowl LVI against the LA Rams.

GLOSSARY

COVID-19 PANDEMIC (KOH-vid nine-TEEN pan-DEM-ik)—a very contagious, sometimes deadly, virus that spread worldwide in 2020

DRAFT (DRAFT)—when athletes are picked to join sports organizations

INTERCEPTION (in-tur-SEP-shun)—a pass caught by a defensive player

LIGAMENT (LIG-uh-muhnt)—a band of tissue connecting bones

OFFENSIVE (OFF-fens-iv)—part of a team whose job it is to score points

PLAYOFFS (PLAY-awfs)—a series of games a team plays to get to the championship

POVERTY (PAW-vuhr-tee)—the state of being poor or without money

RECRUITER (ri-KROOT-uhr)—a person who seeks out players for college or professional sports programs

REHAB (REE-hab)—exercises for healing after an injury

ROOKIE (RUK-ee)—a first-year player

SACK (SAK)—when a defensive player tackles the opposing quarterback

WILD CARD (WILD CARD)—a team that advances to the playoffs without winning its division

READ MORE

Abdo, Kenny. *Cincinnati Bengals*. Minneapolis: Fly!, an imprint of Abdo Zoom, 2022.

Coleman, Ted. *Cincinnati Bengals All-Time Greats*. Mendota Heights, MN: Press Box Books, an imprint of Press Room Editions, 2022.

Fishman, Jon M. *Joe Burrow*. Minneapolis: Lerner Publications, 2022.

Wyner, Zach. *Cincinnati Bengals*. New York: AV2, 2020.

INTERNET SITES

Bengals.com: Joe Burrow
bengals.com/team/players-roster/joe-burrow/

NFL.com: Joe Burrow
nfl.com/players/joe-burrow/

The Joe Burrow Hunger Relief Fund
appalachianohio.org/grow/funds/fund-profiles/joeburrow/

INDEX

AUTHOR BIO

Mari Bolte is the author and editor of many books for children, ranging from video games to cute animals to sports stars. A lifelong Green Bay Packers fan, she lives in the frozen tundra and dreams of Lambeau leaps.